Smashing the Stereotypes: What Does It Mean to Be Gay, Lesbian, Bisexual, or Transgender?

The Gallup's Guide to Modern Gay, Lesbian, & Transgender Lifestyle
Series List

Smashing the Stereotypes: What Does It Mean to Be Gay, Lesbian, Bisexual, or Transgender?

by Jaime A. Seba

Mason Crest Publishers

MASON CREST PUBLISHERS INC.
370 Reed Road
Broomall, Pennsylvania 19008
(866)MCP-BOOK (toll free)
www.masoncrest.com

First Printing
9 8 7 6 5 4 3 2 1

Library of Congress Cataloging-in-Publication Data

Seba, Jaime.
 Smashing the stereotypes : what does it mean to be gay, lesbian, bisexual, or transgender? / by Jaime A. Seba.
    p. cm. — (The Gallup's guide to modern gay, lesbian, & transgender lifestyle)
 Includes bibliographical references and index.
 ISBN 978-1-4222-1755-9   ISBN 978-1-4222-1758-0 (series)
 ISBN 978-1-4222-1874-7 (pbk.) ISBN 978-1-4222-1863-1 (pbk. series)
 1. Gay men—Juvenile literature. 2. Lesbians—Juvenile literature. 3. Bisexuals—Juvenile literature. 4. Transgender people—Juvenile literature. I. Title.
 HQ76.S43 2011
 306.76'8—dc22
                                2010026503

Produced by Harding House Publishing Service, Inc.
www.hardinghousepages.com
Interior design by MK Bassett-Harvey.
Cover design by Torque Advertising + Design.
Printed in the USA by Bang Printing.

4913 7242 3/12

PICTURE CREDITS

Aplet, Mark; Fotolia: p. 57
Arrow Studio, Fotolia: p. 59
Centers for Disease Control: p. 26
Creative Commons: p. 11, 32, 42, 47
Francis, Glenn; www.PacificProDigital.com; Creative Commons: p. 50
Judy Tejero Photography; Fotolia: p. 12
Kokkinis, Konstantinos; Fotolia: p. 60
Nastynegs, Fotolia: p. 34
NET Television: p. 24

Nguyen, Marie-Lan; Creative Commons: p. 16
1000 Demonios, Fotolia: p. 41
PR Photos: p. 39
Thelmadatter, Creative Commons: p. 29
Wilson, Bill; Creative Commons: p. 49

Contents

Introduction

We are both individuals and community members. Our differences define individuality; our commonalities create a community. Some differences, like the ability to run swiftly or to speak confidently, can make an individual stand out in a way that is viewed as beneficial by a community, while the group may frown upon others. Some of those differences may be difficult to hide (like skin color or physical disability), while others can be hidden (like religious views or sexual orientation). Moreover, what some communities or cultures deem as desirable differences, like thinness, is a negative quality in other contemporary communities. This is certainly the case with sexual orientation and gender identity, as explained in *Homosexuality Around the World*, one of the volumes in this book series.

Often, there is a tension between the individual (individual rights) and the community (common good). This is easily visible in everyday matters like the right to own land versus the common good of building roads. These cases sometimes result in community controversy and often are adjudicated by the courts.

An even more basic right than property ownership, however, is one's gender and sexuality. Does the right of gender expression trump the concerns and fears of a community or a family or a school? *Feeling Wrong in Your Own Body*, as the author of that volume suggests, means confronting, in the most personal way, the tension between individuality and community. And, while a community, family, and school have the right (and obligation) to protect its children, does the notion of property rights extend to controlling young adults' choice as to how they express themselves in terms of gender or sexuality?

Changes in how a community (or a majority of the community) thinks about an individual right or responsibility often precedes changes in the law enacted by legislatures or decided by courts. And for these changes to occur, individuals (sometimes working in small groups) often defied popular opinion, political pressure, or religious beliefs. Some of these trends are discussed in *A New Generation of Homosexuality*. Every generation (including yours!) stands on the accomplishments of our ancestors and in *Gay and Lesbian Role Models* you'll be reading about some of them.

One of the most pernicious aspects of discrimination on the basis of sexual orientation is that "homosexuality" is a stigma that can be hidden (see the volume about *Homophobia*). While some of my generation (I was your age in the early 1960s) think that life is so much easier being "queer" in the age of the Internet, Gay-Straight Alliances, and Ellen, in reality, being different in areas where difference matters is *always* difficult. Coming Out, as described in the volume of the same title, is always challenging—for both those who choose to come out and for the friends and family they trust with what was once a hidden truth. Being healthy means being honest—at least to yourself. Having supportive friends and family is most important, as explained in *Being Gay, Staying Healthy*.

Sometimes we create our own "families"—persons bound together by love and identity but not by name or bloodline. This is quite common in gay communities today as it was several generations ago. Forming families or small communities based on rejection by the larger community can also be a double-edged sword. While these can be positive, they may also turn into prisons of conformity. Does being lesbian, for example, mean everyone has short hair, hates men, and drives (or rides on) a motorcycle? *What Does It Mean to Be Gay, Lesbian, Bisexual, or Transgender?* "smashes" these and other stereotypes.

Another common misconception is that "all gay people are alike"—a classic example of a stereotypical statement. We may be drawn together because of a common prejudice or oppression, but we should not forfeit our individuality for the sake of the safety of a common identity, which is one of the challenges shown in *Gay People of Color: Facing Prejudices, Forging Identities*.

Coming out to who *you* are is just as important as having a group or "family" within which to safely come out. Becoming knowledgeable about these issues (through the books in this series and the other resources to which they will lead), feeling good about yourself, behaving safely, actively listening to others *and* to your inner spirit—all this will allow you to fulfill your promise and potential.

James T. Sears, PhD
Consultant

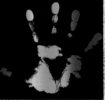

chapter 1

What Are Stereotypes?

Ed Wesley remembers what it was like before he came out and told the world he's gay. He felt alone and out of place. All he knew about the lesbian, gay, bisexual, and *transgender* (LGBT) community was the characters he'd seen on television and the way gay people were shown in the media. To him, it seemed like all gay men squealed like girls, were obsessed with body image, wore women's clothing, and talked with a lisp.

That wasn't Ed.

"I'm not a skinny little gay boy," he said. "I'm a big guy. I'm not like the characters they show on television or on the news. So for a little while, that made me wonder if I was gay, because I didn't fit the way I was supposed to. I thought I was supposed to be something else. It was confusing."

What's That Mean?

Transgender has to do with identifying with a different gender than the one that corresponds with a person's sex at birth. In other words, a person who was born male would have a female identity; a person born female would have a male identity.

When Ed finally realized that being gay didn't mean he would have to fit into a set image, he felt more comfortable with himself and his sexual identity. He was able to embrace his homosexuality and come out. But he isn't the only gay person who has been confused by the stereotypes that exist in modern culture.

According to the *Merriam-Webster* dictionary, a stereotype is a **standardized** mental picture that is held in common by members of a group and that represents an oversimplified opinion, prejudiced attitude, or uncritical judgment. Put more simply, it's when someone looks at an entire group of people and defines all of them in the same way, by just a few characteristics. In most cases, stereotypes are negative or highlight only the most extreme elements of the group. They overlook the more complicated aspects of the individual people in the group.

What's That Mean?

Something that is **standardized** is made to conform to a set of rules.

Generalizations are vague opinions not based on specific facts.

"I'm much more than just a gay stereotype," said Wesley. "All people are more than the **generalizations** we sometimes give them. I hate when people do it to me, but I realize that I do it to other people, too."

Stereotypes exist for many different groups. Thinking that all black people can dance well, or all Japanese students are geniuses, are examples of stereotypes. Stereotypes aren't necessarily bad things. There's nothing wrong with dancing well or being very smart. The problem comes when someone ignores an individual, and instead only thinks about the stereotypes.

And sometimes stereotypes can be truly harmful. In 1999, the cartoon character Speedy Gonzales was

Speedy Gonzales presents a stereotyped—and incorrect—image of Mexicans.

This is the stereotype image we often have in our minds when we hear the word "nerd."

taken off the air because many experts believed that he and his fellow mice characters perpetuated stereotypes of Mexicans. According to this stereotype, all Mexicans have thick accents, and are often drunk and always lazy. Some people felt cancelling the cartoon was extreme, but for many children, Speedy was their introduction to Mexican culture—and it meant they started out life with a warped (and untrue) perception of Mexicans.

"Stereotypes hurt people," said Brian Jones, an out gay black man. "Whether they're based on race or culture or sexual orientation. Even if it's meant as a joke or just to be funny, some people take it seriously. And when that happens, the problems can start, because some people don't realize that it's a joke or even a stereotype. They think it's fact and true."

EXTRA INFO

You may think that gender and sexuality mean the same thing—but actually, they are two different things. According to the World Health Organization:

"Sex" refers to the biological and physiological characteristics that define men and women.

"Gender" refers to the socially constructed roles, behaviors, activities, and attributes that a society considers appropriate for men and women.

To put it another way: "Male" and "female" are sex categories, while "masculine" and "feminine" are gender categories.

Aspects of sex will not vary substantially between different human societies, while aspects of gender may vary greatly.

Examples of Sex Characteristics
- Women menstruate while men do not.
- Men have testicles while women do not.
- Women have developed breasts that can produce milk for babies, while men have not.
- Men generally have heavier bones than women.

Examples of Gender Characteristics
- In the United States (and most other countries), women earn significantly less money than men for similar work.
- In much of the Western world, women can wear dresses while men do not.
- In Saudi Arabia men are allowed to drive cars while women are not.
- In most of the world, women do more housework than men.

When it comes to sexual orientation, you can be attracted to the same sex and yet still identify with the same gender as your biological sex. Or you can be attracted to the opposite sex and yet identify with a different gender than your biological sex.

When people think of the LGBT communities, they often immediately envision the many stereotypes that have become common in entertainment and the media. Many people, especially those who don't personally know any LGBT individuals, think all gay people conform to stereotypes. This often begins with the belief that gay men behave like women, and gay women behave like men.

Drag queens often take part in Gay Pride parades, contributing to an image for gay people that is actually far from typical for the average gay person.

"When I saw what I thought gay people were—what the stereotypes were—I was scared because I didn't fit into it," said openly gay writer Fred Carlton. "I thought I would have to change who I was just so I could be gay. And that doesn't make any sense at all. I thought I was going to have to be more like a woman, and I don't want to be a woman! I can be sensitive and creative, while still being a man."

Stereotypes of the LGBT community often confuse a person's sexual orientation with his or her gender identity. When someone is physically attracted to a member of the same sex, that is his or her sexual orientation. It doesn't mean gay men are more feminine than straight men, nor are gay women more masculine than straight women.

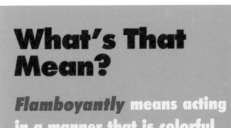

What's That Mean?

Flamboyantly means acting in a manner that is colorful and a bit outrageous.

To be *butch* is to be masculine in dress and appearance.

But sometimes stereotypes are true. After all, they come from somewhere, even when they become exaggerated. Many people know or have seen *flamboyantly* gay men or tough *butch* lesbians. Gay pride festivals and parades showcase some of the most extreme, stereotyped members of the community.

But the mistake many people make is to think that these stereotypes describe what *all* gay people are or how they behave.

"Stereotypes are what keep people in the closet," Wesley said. "They aren't what we can be or even what we want to be."

As was the case when Wesley was coming out, stereotypes can be confusing to individuals who are questioning their sexual orientation, especially if they don't know any gay or lesbian people. They may already feel out of place among their peers, and they may not feel that they fit in with gay stereotypes, either. They may be embarrassed to associate themselves with some of the **disparaging** stereotypes that have been linked to gay people.

I don't want someone to look at me and just see a black man or just see a gay man," said Jones. "I want them to see Brian, the person I am. I don't swish when I walk. I'm not a rapper. I do some things that are considered 'black' and I do things that are considered 'gay.' But I also do hundreds of other things. I'm more than just a stereotype."

FIND OUT MORE ON THE INTERNET

Inaccurate and Overly Hostile Stereotypes
www.colorado.edu/conflict/peace/problem/stereoty.htm

We Don't Need Gay Stereotypes
www.guardian.co.uk/commentisfree/2010/feb/06/gay-
stereotypes-rights-venues

READ MORE ABOUT IT

Stanger, Charles. *Stereotypes and Prejudice: Key Readings.*
Philadelphia, Penn.: Psychology Press, 2000.

Streitmatter, Rodger. *From "Perverts" to "Fab Five": The Media's
Changing Depiction of Gay Men and Lesbians.* New York:
Routledge, 2009.

chapter 2

Stereotypes of Gay Men

In the 1995 movie *Clueless*, a character describes a gay classmate as "a disco-dancing, Oscar Wilde-reading, Streisand ticket-holding friend of Dorothy." His friend adds, "He does like to shop . . . and the boy can dress."

They were referring to some of the most common stereotypes associated with gay men—they enjoy dancing at clubs, behave like openly gay nineteenth-century writer Oscar Wilde, and are fans of singer Barbara Streisand and actress Judy Garland, who portrayed Dorothy in *The Wizard of Oz*. It's also said that gay men enjoy shopping and have an excellent sense of style and fashion.

"We all love Cher. We all love Marilyn Monroe," said Tom Boller, an openly gay architect in New York City. "We prance and mince and clap our hands and say things like, 'That's fabulous!' That's what people think. And when you look on television or [in] movies, that's what it seems like. But that's not how it really is. I play soccer every weekend. I don't know anything about Marilyn Monroe. I never say, 'fabulous.'"

There are also certain occupations that tend to be thought of as "gay." Hairdressers, interior decorators, florists, dancers, and stage actors are all jobs commonly thought to be filled by gay men. These stereotypes not only generalize all gay people, but also the straight people who choose these careers.

"People assume that if you're a male ballet dancer, you're gay," said Zach Hench, a straight professional dancer from Philadelphia. "And I think it's quite silly because let's think about it—you are working around beautiful women all day that are half naked. It's a great job for straight guys."

While it's true that gay men may be drawn to the creative arts, where

Oscar Wilde was a nineteenth-century British author known for his flamboyant homosexuality.

personal expression is encouraged and people tend to be more open-minded, the expectation that all people in these jobs are gay, or the idea that these are the only jobs that can be held by gay people, make them unrealistic stereotypes. "I know gay lawyers, gay doctors, gay teachers, gay coaches, gay athletes, gay accountants," said Boller. "We're not all wedding planners and pet groomers. Those are just the silly stereotypes that people see in movies and on TV. But if they don't know any actual gay people, then they don't know better."

Hollywood has often been guilty of presenting and even causing stereotypes. Countless movies show flamboyantly gay characters who often get laughs by showing all the most common stereotypes. The popular sitcom *Will & Grace* was a huge step forward for gay and lesbian people on television, but many felt the show didn't do a good enough job of showing diversity in the gay community. The gay characters of Will and Jack were often obsessed with appearances, money, and fashion. They made jokes about lesbians, bisexuals, and transgender people,

What's That Mean?

A *caricature* is an exaggerated representation of a character, usually created to make people laugh.

An *activist* is someone who takes action on behalf of a particular cause.

showing how the gay community can often be as guilty of stereotyping as the rest of the world. Jack in particular was a **caricature** of gay stereotypes, an out-of-work actor who worshiped Cher and used his own language of pop culture references as he dished out catty jibes to his friends.

"I don't care if he's rich or poor, fat or thin," said Jack, describing his ideal mate. "As long as he's rich and thin."

Such characters are common in popular culture. Television, movies, and theater frequently feature prancing, limp-wristed gay men who fill the role of the stylish sidekick.

"Those flaming gay characters are funny. I laugh at them!" said Todd Ramos, a gay **activist**. "And I don't think there's anything wrong with them when it comes to entertainment. But the problem is that some people think that's what all gay people are like, or when they think that's *all* gay people are."

Some stereotypes can also be very damaging in other ways. In the 1980s, due to the high number of homosexual men infected with HIV, the virus that causes AIDS, people often considered it a gay disease. That led to the stereotype that all gay men have AIDS.

"That's probably one of the worst," Ramos said. "I remember when I told my mother I was gay, and that was the first thing she said. She was scared I

Although the TV show Will & Grace *was considered to be groundbreaking in many ways for the gay community, it also helped perpetuate some gay stereotypes.*

would get AIDS. And it didn't come from a hateful place. It was just because she didn't know any better. She believed what she saw on television."

Another negative effect of stereotypes is that they are difficult to escape. This was the case for Sean Hayes, who played Jack on *Will & Grace* for the show's eight seasons and came out publicly in 2010. As one of the increasing number of openly gay actors in Hollywood, Hayes was then faced with the question of whether he would be able to play straight characters. The stereotypically flamboyant Jack, his most famous and recognized role, had come to define his identity.

Hayes was in the center of public controversy in April 2010, when *Newsweek's* Ramin Setoodah reviewed his performance in the Broadway stage play *Promises, Promises*, in which Hayes played a straight leading man. In his review, Setoodah wrote that Hayes's history of having played a gay character, and his private sexual orientation, made it difficult to believe he was a straight character in the play.

"Hayes is among Hollywood's best verbal slap-stickers, but his sexual orientation is part of who he is, and also part of his charm," Setoodah wrote. "But frankly, it's weird seeing Hayes play straight."

Immediately, people reacted strongly to the controversial viewpoint, particularly because Setoodah himself is gay. Hayes's co-star in the play, actress

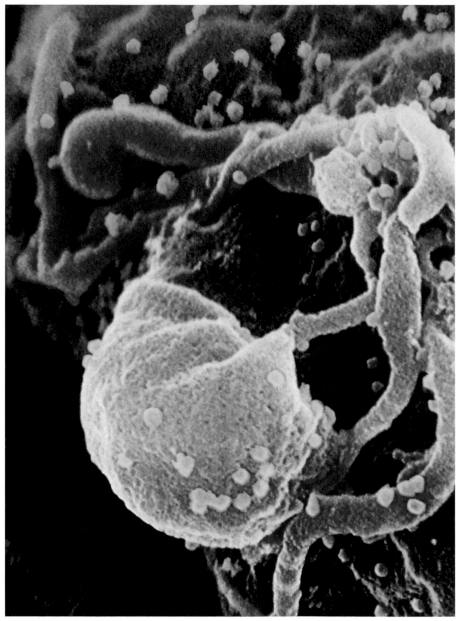

The HIV virus shown here was mistakenly considered a gay man's problem. In reality, however, microbes do not recognize stereotypes, and this virus is as dangerous to straights as it is to gays.

Kristin Chenoweth, was furious at what she called a "**homophobic**" article. She responded with a written statement defending her on-stage love interest.

"This article offends me because I am a human being, a woman and a Christian," she wrote.

For example, there was a time when Jewish actors had to change their names because anti-Semites thought no Jew could convincingly play a Gentile. Setoodeh even goes so far as to justify his knee-jerk homophobic reaction to gay actors by accepting and endorsing that "as viewers, we are molded by a society obsessed with dissecting sexuality, starting with the locker room torture in junior high school." Really? We want to maintain and **proliferate** the same kind of bullying that makes children cry and in some recent cases have even taken their own lives?

What's That Mean?

Something that is **homophobic** supports the fear and hatred of gay people.

To **proliferate** means to increase and multiply.

Soon numerous stage and screen actors and writers joined Chenowith's outrage, including Oscar-winning screenwriter Dustin Lance Black. The Gay and Lesbian Alliance Against Defamation (GLAAD), which monitors the way LGBT people are portrayed

What's That Mean?

Effeminate refers to a man who looks or acts in ways that are considered "feminine."

in entertainment and media, also expressed disappointment with the homophobic attitude.

"We must move beyond stereotypes," GLAAD President Jarrett Barrios wrote about the article. "As a gay man, Setoodah should know that not all gay men are *effeminate*, nor are all les-

EXTRA INFO

A Bear is LGBT slang for a segment of the gay community that doesn't exactly fit many people's stereotypes of how gay men should look and behave. Bears tend to be big men with facial hair, and they project an image of traditional masculinity in the way they dress and carry themselves. Much more likely to be seen in jeans, boots, and a flannel shirt than the latest fashion, Bears have a "regular guy" image that contradicts the stereotype that all gay men are somehow "feminine." Bears are masculine-identified men who happen to like (usually) other masculine-identified men. Most Bears are proud to call themselves gay men and to represent the gay community to the world in their own unique and "furry" way.

bians masculine. Actors are hired to play a part and their sexual orientation should have no bearing on how well they can do so."

Not only did Setoodah's perspective imply that gay actors should be limited to playing only gay roles, but it also indicated that heterosexual men couldn't behave like Hayes and still be considered straight. This is what can make stereotypes so damaging. They can make people afraid of being who they really are. Stereotypes are just another way of separating people into categories of what's "normal" and what's not.

"Bears" took part in a Gay Pride parade in Mexico City.

"Seriously, why can't straight men dress well and like Madonna?" said Joe Duarte, a straight man who works with many gay men in the travel industry. "People think I'm gay all the time. I consider it a compliment. Gay guys I know look good, and they are nice, friendly guys. So I'm not insulted. But it's crazy to say that one way of talking or dressing or even gesturing is gay or straight. We're all just people. Why can't people just be who they are?"

FIND OUT MORE ON THE INTERNET

Does Television's Gay Influx Promote Stereotypes?
www.newsweek.com/2009/11/11/kings-of-queens.html

Is There Such a Thing as "Sounding" Gay?
speech-language-therapy.com/codemix.htm

READ MORE ABOUT IT

Gideonse, Ted. *From Boys to Men: Gay Men Write About Growing Up*. New York: Carroll & Graf Publishers, 2006.

Pascoe, C. J. Dude, *You're A Fag: Masculinity and Sexuality in High School*. Berkeley, Calif.: University of California Press, 2007.

chapter 3

Stereotypes of Lesbians

She plays softball. She must be a lesbian.

That was a common attitude when a photo surfaced in 2010 of Supreme Court nominee Elena Kagan playing softball. The picture, which simply showed her holding a bat standing over home plate, prompted rumors that she was gay. While her sexual orientation should be irrelevant to her competency as a judge, the bigger issue was the stereotype that simply playing the sport immediately means a woman is a lesbian.

"I think it's unfortunate," Lisa Fernandez, a three-time Olympic gold medalist and assistant coach at the University of California Los Angeles, said of the stereotype. "It's part of our game."

Jessica Mendoza won two Olympic gold medals, but when she first began playing softball, she was surprised to learn that it was considered a lesbian sport. "There were always comments about sexuality being associated with sports," she said. "And it caught me off guard a few times."

Holly Elander, a senior who plays softball at Santa Monica High School in California, also recognizes the stereotype associated with her sport. And she sees teammates **compensating** for that. "You see a lot of girls wearing makeup, a lot of girls with their hair really pretty because you can definitely tell they still want to look pretty and probably go

What's That Mean?

Compensating means making up for something by trying harder or going further in the opposite direction than might otherwise be expected.

Stereotypically, one member of a lesbian couple has been more "butch" or masculine, while the other has played a more feminine role. In actuality, there are many variations of lesbian relationships—just as there an equal number of variations in heterosexual relationships.

EXTRA INFO

Gay women who dress and act in traditional feminine ways are called "lipstick lesbians" in gay slang, and the term has caught on with the general public. Many straight people seem to be fascinated with the idea of a glamorous-looking gay woman. Lipstick lesbians don't look or act like the tired, old "a woman who wants to be a man" stereotype of lesbians—they can have just as much fun with fashion and makeup and "pretty things" as any other woman. Some lipstick lesbians are attracted to other feminine women, some like their girlfriends to be butch. Hey, it's a free country!

against those stereotypes that were pinned against them," she said.

In addition to playing softball, stereotypes associated with lesbians are linked to other physical characteristics traditionally considered to be masculine. Things like short hair, a "tough" walk, and talents in fixing cars and home repairs are often connected with gay women.

"People always make the assumption that I'm handy just because I'm a lesbian," said Callie Franks, who came out when she was in college. "When I first realized I was gay, I tried to fill those stereotypes. I cut my hair really short. I became an in-your-face feminist. But that wasn't me. The real me isn't tough.

As this couple demonstrated on their wedding day, no rule says that both members of a lesbian couple can't be equally feminine.

I'm scared of spiders. The whole hard-core dyke thing was just a phase. But the lesbian thing is here to stay."

By using the term "dyke," Franks demonstrated a way in which many people in the LGBT communities fight stereotypes—by taking back once-derogatory terms and eliminating the negativity. Some lesbians have adopted "dyke" as a way of referring to themselves. In the same way, gay people have claimed the word "queer" as a term defining anyone who identifies with a sexual orientation or gender role that is outside what people consider "normal."

"When we use words like 'queer' or 'dyke' or even 'fairy' and 'queen,' we take the power away from the people who use them negatively," Franks said. "We make them our own words, and then suddenly they aren't so bad any more. We turn those stereotypes around."

Lesbians are also generally dropped into two categories—butch women, who are given the male role, and femmes, who are often considered to be more like straight women. Limiting people to two such narrow roles overlooks the things that make each individual unique.

"If you have long hair, if you have makeup and dress in a certain way, then you can't be a lesbian," said Mary Jo Kane, director of the Tucker Center for

Research on Girls & Women in Sport at the University of Minnesota. "These are the traditionally female characteristics. And they are false."

FIND OUT MORE ON THE INTERNET

Pssst. The Girl's Guide to Lesbian Stereotypes
jezebel.com/5205953/pssst-the-girls-guide-to-lesbian-cliches--stereotypes

Styled "Out": The Lesbian Look (from LOGO online)
www.afterellen.com/blog/emilyhartl/styled-out-the-lesbian-stereotype

READ MORE ABOUT IT

Abate, Michelle Ann. *Tomboys: A Literary and Cultural History.* Philadelphia, Penn.: Temple University Press, 2008.

Faderman, Lillian, *Odd Girls and Twilight Lovers: A History of Lesbian Life in Twentieth Century America.* New York: Penguin Books, 1998.

chapter 4

Stereotypes of Bisexual People

Gay and lesbian people often face stereotypes and discrimination from the world. But within the LGBT community, stereotypes also exist.

Bisexual people are often thought of as being different from "real" gay people. Many gays and lesbians believe bisexuals are just confused or haven't made a decision to come out as completely gay.

"Isn't that just a rest stop on the road to 'homo'?" said gay title character Will on the sitcom, *Will & Grace*, when discussing the concept.

That attitude is not uncommon. Bisexuality is often considered something young people try when they are in college, as they experiment with sexuality or question their orientation. While this may be the case for some, it is also unfairly judgmental of individuals who are trying to be themselves in what should be an accepting community.

"The oppression that bisexuals face is wrong, whether it is coming from the gay and lesbian community or the heterosexual community," said Lowell Kane, program coordinator of Texas A&M University's LGBT Center. "**Horizontal hostility** within the GLBT community is very troubling and certainly creates a roadblock on the path toward equity. I believe that many of the misconceptions about bisexuality and bisexual people can be cleared up with education, visibility, and a willingness to openly discuss sexuality in a civil way."

Bisexual people are physically attracted to both men and women. Some researchers believe that this is much more common than most people realize or acknowledge. Broadway star Megan Mullally, who played Karen on the television show *Will & Grace*, has spoken publicly about the fact that she is attracted to both women and men, even though the majority of her serious relationships have been with men.

"I consider myself bisexual, and my philosophy is, everyone **innately** is," she said.

What's That Mean?

Negative feeling among people within the same minority group is referred to as *horizontal hostility*.

Innately refers to characteristics that are most basic to a person, those traits with which they were born.

Megan Mullally has publically identified herself as being bisexual and has spoken out on behalf of this group of people.

The idea that bisexual people are confused about their sexual orientation can make challenging personal times even more difficult. Bisexual people may not be accepted by the straight community because they are involved in same-sex relationships but also not accepted by the gay community because they still are seen as partly heterosexual.

"Within the GLBT community, there is almost a social **hierarchy**," said Casey Beck, who identified as bisexual while a student in college. "Some homosexuals believe they are somehow better than bisexual and transgendered, somehow socially more adept, seen as less questioning, and more sure of their identity. But questioning is something we should be doing, and we should be helping students discover their sexuality and live the lives they want."

Beck eventually recognized that he was gay, and he no longer dates women. But he still recalls how difficult it was to be the "B" in the LGBT community. He felt pressure to prove that he belonged—just as he often felt when he tried to fit in with the heterosexual community.

What's That Mean?

A *hierarchy* organizes things-or people-in layers of importance, with those at the top having the most status or importance.

To *legitimize* something means to make it acceptable to most people.

"When I tell people I'm gay, the reaction is different," Beck said. "When I used to identify as bi, there's a game of twenty questions with an extra burden to explain and **legitimize** your sexuality."

Beck also had to deal with the stereotype that bisexual people are more likely to cheat than other people. This is often mistakenly assumed because bisexual people are attracted to both genders, which theoretically means they could be attracted to anyone.

"People always seem to think that if you're bisexual, then you can't be in a monogamous relationship," said Sara Schneider. "As if just because you

If someone is bisexual, he or she may feel caught in the middle between the sexes, neither one thing or another—but again, sexual orientation and gender are not the same thing!

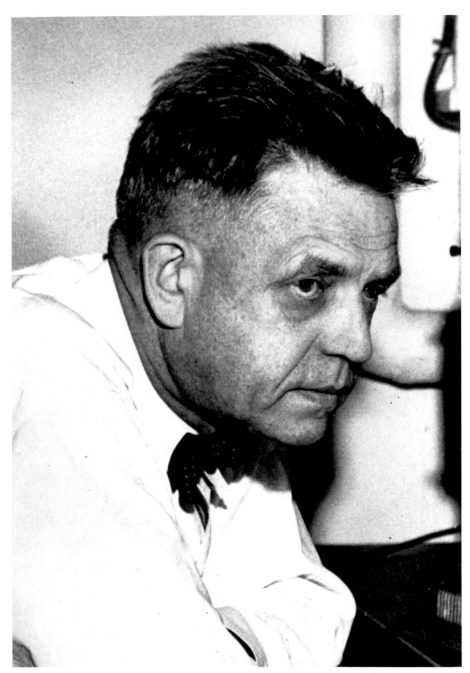

Alfred Kinsey's research into sexuality broke many of the stereotypes that had previously existed.

could be attracted to another man or woman, you're going to act on it. But that's like saying that all gay people cheat. Or that all straight people cheat. The fact is, cheaters cheat—gay, lesbian, bisexual, or straight."

Schneider came out as a lesbian in high school, but when she was twenty-two, she met a young man

EXTRA INFO

The pioneering sex researcher Alfred Kinsey broke from popular thinking on sexuality in the 1950s, theorizing that bisexuality was much more common than previously thought. Kinsey is probably famous for his sexual-orientation scale, which represents exclusive heterosexuality with a zero and exclusive homosexuality with a six — some degree of bisexuality exists in people whose numbers are 1 to 5 on the scale. In the 1980s Kinsey's scale was updated by researcher Eli Coleman. Coleman's research broke new ground in understanding human sexuality, showing that while some people identify as either gay or straight consistently throughout their lives, a sizeable proportion of people do not. Many rate themselves as bisexual on questions of desire (or near a three on Kinsey's scale) but maintain exclusive gay or straight relationships. In addition, some people identify as a certain sexual identity at one point in their lives, and as another later on. In other words, sexual behavior and identity are not written in stone, and may shift as we encounter new people or life circumstances.

whom she considered her soul mate. Even after twenty-five years of marriage, however, she still considered herself bisexual.

"I'm married to a man, but that doesn't mean I'm straight," she said. "People really don't understand that. And it doesn't mean I would have a relationship with anyone other than my husband, man or woman. But I know I could have fallen in love with a woman and decided to spend my life with her. To me, it's about the person. If there's a connection in your heart and in your soul, then that's what matters. In my case, that's where the physical attraction comes from. I don't think everyone is like me. Some people are, some people aren't.

"I understand why it confuses people. Not everyone gets it or even agrees with it. That's okay. It would be easier for them if I were one thing, if I would stand up and say, 'Yes, I'm straight.' But I don't think anyone should be something they're not, just because that's what someone else labels them."

What's That Mean?

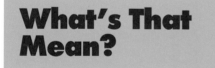

A *spectrum* is a wide range of behaviors and choices.

As people like Lowell Kane continue to spread awareness and a message of acceptance toward bisexual people through LGBT organizations, he hopes that there will be more of a recognition that bisexuality is not a sign of confusion. In fact, it's likely much more common than most people realize.

"Current research suggests that sexuality is more of a fluid **spectrum** than the rigid socially constructed identities of gay, lesbian, straight, bisexual," said Kane. "These recent models of sexuality show that a large percentage (more than 30 percent) of any given population may have thoughts or feelings that fall along the bisexual spectrum, but not all will identify as bisexual because current society frowns upon any non-heterosexual orientation.

FIND OUT MORE ON THE INTERNET

American Institute of Bisexuality
www.bisexual.org/

Human Sexuality: Bisexuality
www.religioustolerance.org/bisexuality.htm

READ MORE ABOUT IT

Baumgardner, Jennifer. *Look Both Ways: Bisexual Politics.* New York: Farrar, Straus, and Giroux, 2007.

Steinman, Erich W. *Bisexuality in the Lives of Men: Facts and Fictions.* New York: Harrington Park Press, 2001.

chapter 5

Stereotypes of Transgender People

A group of students gathered at Penn State University to discuss some of the stereotypes that impact the lesbian, gay, bisexual, and transgender communities. During the meeting, they listed terms such as "shim," "it," and "tranny" on white marker board.

These are words often used for transgender people. They are the result of the stereotype that transgender people are weird, strange, or confused about their gender.

Alex Yates, co-president of the student group that hosted the meeting, drew a diagram on the white board showing two overlapping bell curves representing masculinity and femininity.

"A man and a woman can be more alike than two women or two men," he said, because when following the properties of a bell curve, most people fall into the middle,.

Lex Shaw, a sophomore who participated in the discussion, said she thinks gender roles are created

With the growing movement for recognition and rights for gays, transgenders are forming their own pride movement as well, which includes their own symbol.

Stereotypes of Transgender People 47

by society, when people are "pushing boys to sports and pushing girls to play with dolls."

The term "transgender" generally refers to anyone who is gender-variant, meaning they don't conform to traditional gender roles. In other words, they don't fit in with gender stereotypes. This can include men who prefer to wear women's clothing, as well as people who decide to medically transition to the opposite gender through sexual reassignment surgery.

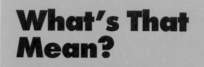

What's That Mean?

An **advocate** is someone who sticks up for another person or group of people.

Issues surrounding gender identity can be very complicated and difficult to understand, even for the individual experiencing them. It becomes much simpler to use stereotypes to define all people who fall under the umbrella of the transgender group.

"I've worked with so many trans people, and I still don't think I understand the many distinctions and differences," said Todd Ramos, an **advocate** for LGBT rights. "But it really doesn't matter if I completely understand. What matters is that I respect people and don't try to shove my beliefs or my definitions on to them. The bottom line is that what someone else does has no effect on me. If a woman feels she fits better into the role of a man, then who

Trangendered people are gaining acceptance and openness. San Francisco's Chief Heather Fong (left) is the city's first female chief of police; Theresa Sparks (center) is the city's first ever transgender police commissioner; and Sergeant Stephan Thorne (right) is the first transgender police officer in San Francisco.

am I to argue? I don't understand it, and it's certainly not how I approach the world, but that's not what matters."

Ramos believes that people have a difficult enough time understanding themselves without being influenced by other people's stereotypes and misunderstandings. The British news website *The Guardian* features a regular column written by Juliet Jacques, who was born male but began feeling more comfortable as a female beginning at age ten.

Transvestites are often men who dress as women for the purposes of a performance. In private life, however, they usually conform to masculine gender roles (though they are often gay). A transsexual person, like the person shown here, however, has fully taken on the identity of a gender different from that person's biological sex. A transsexual may opt for surgery to make this identification a biological reality, or he or she may simply live and dress as a member of the opposite sex.

EXTRA INFO

Gender-identity and sexuality terms can be confusing. Transvestites and transsexuals are two terms that are often misused. Several differences exist between people identifying themselves as transvestites and transsexuals, although the exact definitions may vary from person to person. One of the main differences between transvestites and transsexuals regards gender identification. Transvestites do not usually exhibit any discomfort with their biologically determined sex. Transvestite men want to be men; transvestite women want to be women. Many transvestites choose to adopt habits of dress or appearance of the opposite gender, while retaining all physical characteristics of their sex. In contrast, transsexuals believe that they should be or are truly the opposite sex. A transsexual may take action to make chemical or anatomical alterations to their bodies, in order to be more similar to their desired sex. Some may choose to undergo re-assignment surgery that makes their body appear to be like that of the opposite sex. Many transsexuals live their public lives as the opposite sex, preferring to be seen as the sex they wish to be, rather than that which was biologically determined.

"I declared myself gay and a cross-dresser: 'gay' because although I felt attracted to males who were somehow female, I still considered them men; and 'cross-dresser' because it seemed the most innocuous term," Jacques said.

Thinking that transgender people are gay is also a common stereotype. In reality, it's difficult to label sexual orientation when someone isn't certain of his or her gender identity. For example, Jacques had difficulty maintaining relationships with gay men who were uncomfortable with Jacques's more feminine mannerisms.

Some people also consider all transgender people to be drag queens, another common stereotype. Drag queens, or female impersonators, are men who wear dresses and other women's clothing for entertainment purposes. They may lip synch or dance in nightclub shows or at special events, dressing up only for their performances. This is different from most transgender people, who have made a choice to live their lives as the opposite sex.

"Everyone just kind of thinks that all guys who wear dresses are the same, and they're all freaks," Ramos said. "But it's ignorant to just think everyone who's different from you is a freak. Every person is different. If you take a few minutes to try to understand them, you can learn a lot. You can learn a lot about them, but you can also learn a lot about yourself, because we're all different. Being different is actually what makes us all the same."

FIND OUT MORE ON THE INTERNET

About Transgender People
gaylife.about.com/od/transgender/a/transgender.htm

Transgender Stereotypes
etransgender.com/viewtopic.php?f = 1&t = 348

READ MORE ABOUT IT

Brill, Stephanie. *The Transgender Child: A Handbook for Families and Professionals.* San Francisco, Calif.: Cleis Press, 2009.

Girshick, Lori. *Transgender Voices: Beyond Women and Men.* Lebanon, N.H.: University Press of New England, 2008.

chapter 6

Fighting Stereotypes

We can't help our human tendency to put people into categories. As babies, we faced a confusing world filled with an amazing variety of new things. We needed a way to make sense of it all, so one of our first steps in learning about the world around us was to sort things into separate slots in our heads: small furry things that said *meow* were kitties, while larger furry things that said *arf-arf* were doggies; cars went *vroom-vroom*, but trains were longer and go *choo-choo*; little girls looked one way and little boys another; and doctors wore white coats, while police officers wore blue. These were our earliest stereotypes. They were a handy way to make sense of the world; they helped us know what to expect, so that each time we faced a new person or thing, we weren't starting all over again from scratch. But stereotypes become dangerous when we continue to hold onto our mental images despite new evidence. (For instance, as a child you may have decided that all dogs bite—which means that when faced by friendly, harmless dogs, you assume they're dangerous and so you miss out on getting to know all dogs.) Stereotypes are particularly dangerous and destructive when they're directed at persons or groups of persons. That's when they turn into prejudice.

"Every day, we see stereotypes of what it means to be male and female," said Callie Franks, who teaches tolerance to high school students. "Men are supposed to be big and tough. Women are supposed to be mild and sweet.

"Gay people sometimes break those stereotypes, and I think that's often what makes people afraid or uncomfortable. But if we let go of what we think

EXTRA INFO

Sociologists have found that people who are prejudiced toward one group of people also tend to be prejudiced toward other groups. In a study done in 1946, people were asked about their attitudes concerning a variety of ethnic groups, including Danireans, Pirraneans, and Wallonians. The study found that people who were prejudiced toward blacks and Jews also distrusted these other three groups. The catch is that Danireans, Pirraneans, and Wallonians didn't exist! This suggests that prejudice's existence may be rooted within the person who feels prejudice rather than in the group that is feared and hated.

people are supposed to be, and we just let them be who they are, we'll see that it doesn't really matter."

Joe Duarte has experienced these stereotypes first hand. As an attractive, stylish, self-confident, and highly expressive straight man, he's become accustomed to people thinking he's gay just based on the way he looks. After he traded in his company-issued plain black laptop case for a designer leather bag, he was immediately teased by his colleagues.

"My friend said, 'You must be gay. No straight man would carry a bag like that,'" said Duarte, who was born in Brazil and relocated to Canada as a teenager. "But why shouldn't guys want to do things like that? It looks better. And it doesn't make me less of a man.

My bag or my clothes or my hairstyle have nothing to do with what makes a guy a guy."

His friends often refer to him as "metrosexual"—a straight man who is interested in things traditionally linked to gay men, including shopping, fashion, and grooming. The concept, which is becoming more common in large cities and urban areas, challenges the traditional stereotype that men with effeminate qualities are gay. Duarte's statement implies that to be a gay male would mean he was less masculine— but that's another stereotype! Gay males are just as much "guys" as straight males.

And, as actor Alan Cumming wrote on his blog in May 2010, what is wrong with being

A male who is referred to as "metrosexual" is usually a straight man with a keen eye for fashion.

effeminate? "There are loads of straight people in the world who are effeminate," Cumming wrote. "Does . . . society in general have a problem with people who are too *masculine*?"

The stereotypes of what it means to be a man, woman, gay, straight, bisexual, transgender, or anything else limit people from being who they actually are. Practicing tolerance means letting go of those stereotypes and not making assumptions about people.

The Human Rights Campaign (HRC) suggests that individuals and businesses who want to demonstrate tolerance and break down stereotypes should avoid clichés that *marginalize* gay people. In particular, advertising and media often show extremely effeminate gay men or extremely masculine gay women. The HRC also suggests avoiding language references that include only heterosexuals. Examples of this could include a man's "wife" or a woman's "husband" instead of the general "spouse" or "partner."

Even when stereotypes seem like harmless jokes, they can still hurt people. That's why it's important for people to think about the things they say and the assumptions they make. Stereotypes can often be

We need to get past stereotypes and see people simply as people.

hidden in the everyday things people say and think. Keeping an open mind and reconsidering ways of looking at and thinking about different types of people is the first step toward eliminating harmful stereotypes. Getting to know LGBT people for yourself will help replace stereotypes with actual facts and information.

"It's easy to forget sometimes, especially when you hear other people using those words, how damaging they can be," said Franks. "But when we really think about the way we speak or even the way we think about others, we can start to identify ways that

We are each different—and we are all the same!

we can remove stereotypes from our vocabulary and from our minds. We can look at people for who they are, not who we think they're supposed to be."

FIND OUT MORE ON THE INTERNET

Checking on Stereotypes
www.tolerance.org/activity/checking-stereotypes

Examining the Origins of the Most Common Gay Stereotypes
www.helium.com/items/1510044-examining-the-origins-of-the-most-common-gay-stereotypes

READ MORE ABOUT IT

Halpin, Mikki. *It's Your World—If You Don't Like It, Change It: Activism for Teenagers.* New York: Simon Pulse, 2004.

Huegel, Kelly. *GLBTQ: The Survival Guide for Queer and Questioning Teens.* Minneapolis, Minn.: Free Spirit Publishing, 2003.

BIBLIOGRAPHY

Bardin, Brantley. "25 Coolest Women: Megan Mullaly." *The Advocate*, November 23, 1999.

Boone, Marshand. "Television's Gay Characters Aim to Add Diversity, but Unintentionally Reinforce Negative Stereotypes." *The Daily Orange*, November 12, 2003.

Burnham, Caitlin. "Bisexual, Transgender Stereotypes Discussed." *The Daily Collegian,* June 4, 2010.

Cumming, Alan. "The Hate of the Gays." AlanCumming.com, May 13, 2010.

Human Rights Campaign. www.hrc.org (23 May 2010).

Jacques, Juliet. "A Transgender Journey: Part One." *The Guardian*, June 2, 2010.

"Kristin Defends Sean, Takes on *Newsweek*." *The Advocate*, May 7, 2010.

McPhail, Ian. "Saying Good-Bi to Bigotry." *The Battalion*, June 2, 2010.

Merriam-Webster Online. www.merriam-webster.com (5 June 2010).

Peters, Jeremy W. "Coming Out: When Love Dares Speak, and Nobody Listens." *The New York Times*, May 21, 2010.

Setoodeh, Ramin. "Straight Jacket." *Newsweek*, April 26, 2010.

Stossel, John and Binkley, Gena. "Gay Stereotypes: Are They True?" ABC News, September 15, 2006.

Wharton, David and Rohlin, Melissa "Photo Raises Issue of Sexual Orientation in Softball." *Los Angeles Times*, June 2, 2010.

INDEX

ABOUT THE AUTHOR AND THE CONSULTANT

Jaime A. Seba's involvement in LGBT issues began in 2004, when she helped open the doors of the Pride Center of Western New York, which served a community of more than 100,000 people. As head of public education and outreach, she spearheaded one of the East Coast's first crystal methamphetamine awareness and harm reduction campaigns. She also wrote and developed successful grant programs through the Susan G. Komen Breast Cancer Foundation, securing funding for the region's first breast cancer prevention program designed specifically for gay, bisexual, and transgender women. Jaime studied political science at Syracuse University before switching her focus to communications with a journalism internship at the Press & Sun-Bulletin in Binghamton, New York, in 1999. She is currently a freelance writer based in Seattle.

James T. Sears specializes in research in lesbian, gay, bisexual, and transgender issues in education, curriculum studies, and queer history.

His scholarship has appeared in a variety of peer-reviewed journals and he is the author or editor of twenty books and is the Editor of the Journal of LGBT Youth. Dr. Sears has taught curriculum, research, and LGBT-themed courses in the departments of education, sociology, women's studies, and the honors college at several universities, including: Trinity University, Indiana University, Harvard University, Penn State University, the College of Charleston, and the University of South Carolina. He has also been a Research Fellow at Center for Feminist Studies at the University of Southern California, a Fulbright Senior Research Southeast Asia Scholar on sexuality and culture, a Research Fellow at the University of Queensland, a consultant for the J. Paul Getty Center for Education and the Arts, and a Visiting Research Lecturer in Brazil. He lectures throughout the world.